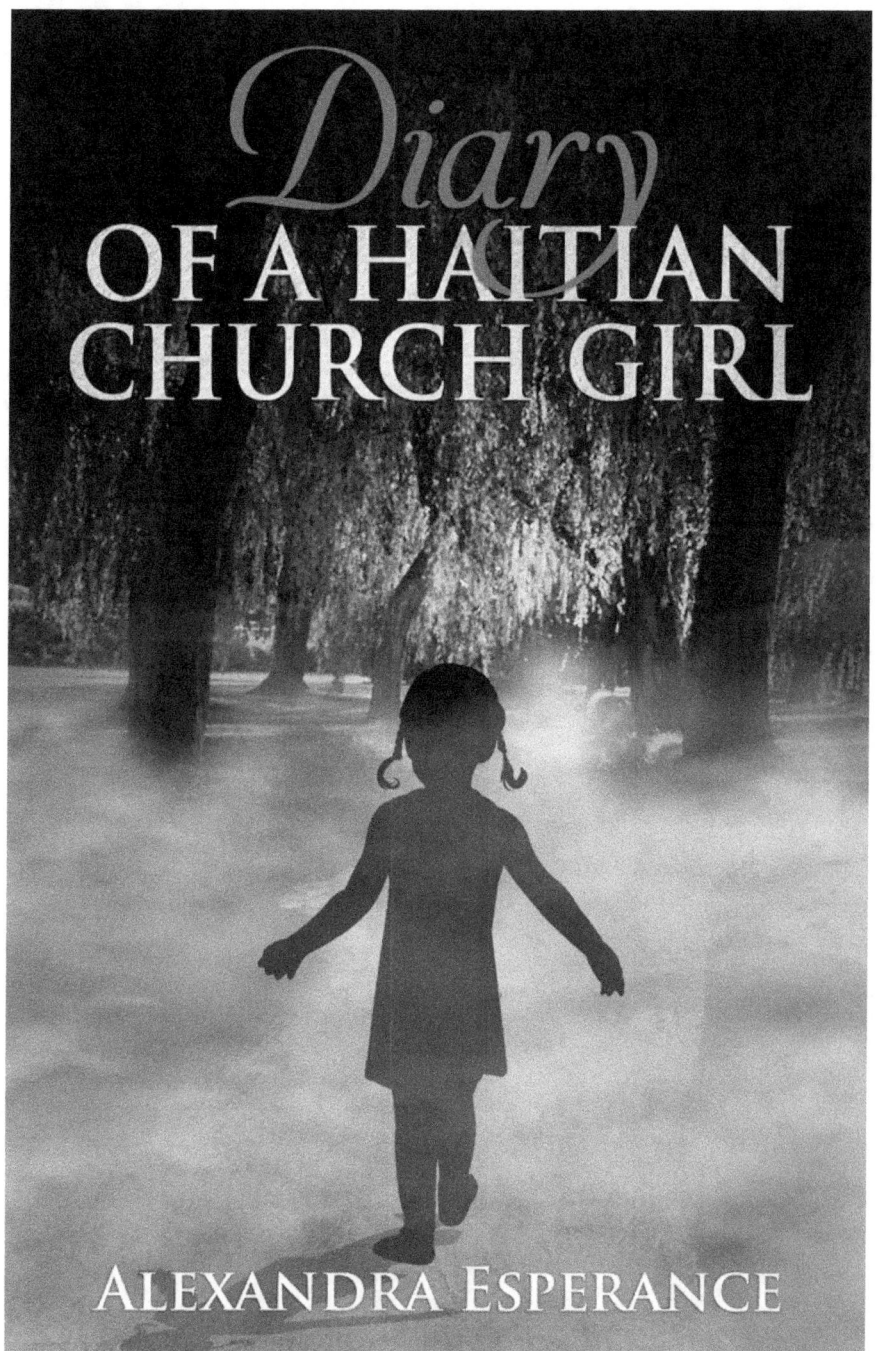

DIARY

OF A

HAITIAN

CHURCH GIRL

Pearly Gates Publishing LLC, Houston, Texas

DIARY OF A HAITIAN CHURCH GIRL

Copyright © 2017
Alexandra Esperance

All Rights Reserved.
No portion of this publication may be reproduced, stored in any electronic system, or transmitted in any form or by any means (electronic, mechanical, photocopy, recording, or otherwise) without written permission from the publisher. Brief quotations may be used in literary reviews.

Unless otherwise stated, all Scripture passages are taken from the New King James Version (NKJV) of the Holy Bible.

ISBN 13: 978-1945117503
ISBN 10: 1945117508
Library of Congress Control Number: 2016960339

For information, contact:
Pearly Gates Publishing LLC
Angela R. Edwards
P.O. Box 62287
Houston, TX 77205
BestSeller@PearlyGatesPublishing.com

DEDICATION

Diary of a Haitian Girl is dedicated to youths of all nations who feel as if they have lost their voice. It is especially dedicated to the Haitian children. This has been written to let you know that what you have been through does not define you.

I pray this book serves as a reminder: We are not God's forgotten children, even if it may feel that way. Although we may feel disowned or suffocated with our mouths taped and unable to speak, there is life after we feel as if we have died.

ACKNOWLEDGMENTS

All honor and praise is given to the Most High God - the inspiration for this book and the One who knew the outcome of my life before I was born. I exalt Him for teaching and allowing me to have a piece of Him inside of me. I exalt Him for waiting for and listening to me, even when I was disobedient to Him. I am grateful for having a purpose for my past mistakes and for making me reusable.

To My Mother, Roselia Forest: I am forever grateful for all that you have done. With all that I put you through, you still decided to stand beside me. I know you did the best you could with what you were given. Thank you for being a praying mother.

To Church of A New Revelation: You are the soil God prepared to have me planted to get to know Him better. You taught me a different way of reaching God. Thank you for not conforming to the traditions of what a church should be, but always allowing God to take first place.

To My Spiritual Father, Pastor Vilner Eugene: The late-night phone calls of encouragement were not in vain. I appreciate your transparency. Thank you for being obedient to God. Without your obedience, I would have continued to be a lost sheep.

To David Vincent: No amount of words can express the gratitude I have towards you. You were definitely God-sent at the right time in my life. Thank you for allowing God to use you so that I am able to see myself the way God sees me.

Last, but not least - to my Family and Friends: Thank you for just being who you are in both good and bad times. To all who were a part of my life and journey, thank you for being an instrument in God's teaching for me.

INTRODUCTION

Many people go through life - hardship after hardship - but can never think back to when the issues of life began. At times, traumatic experiences from our childhood cause the devil to enter our lives and cause things to be out of order. If we do not have a strong foundation from family, we tend to get lost along the way and unable to fulfill the purpose God has created for us.

The devil attacks and tries to strip us of our innocence at a young age. He makes us feel unworthy so that others are not concerned about us. We feel so ashamed about our situation and tend to detach ourselves from others - even if they are there to help us. Then, we start to attach ourselves to *wrong* people - which causes us to continue walking in the wilderness blindly. We become so blinded, we can't see the Promised Land that **God** has created just for us.

DIARY OF A HAITIAN CHURCH GIRL

Imagine spending a week reliving **all** of your past hurt, abandonment, brokenness, anger, and isolation - in the midst of finding your purpose...

I've done just that.

On the pages of *Diary of a Haitian Church Girl*, I am going to share some of my traumatic experiences that led to so many bad choices in my life. As you are reading, I want you to reflect on your life and see what you can learn from it. Ask yourself: *How can I use my past to change the future the devil is **trying** to create?*

Relive my experiences with me. As you are reading, learn from my mistakes, gain strength from my pains, and become wiser from my ignorance.

~ Alexandra Esperance ~

DIARY OF A HAITIAN CHURCH GIRL

DIARY OF A HAITIAN CHURCH GIRL

TABLE OF CONTENTS

DEDICATION	VI
ACKNOWLEDGMENTS	VII
INTRODUCTION	X
MOLESTATION	2
BROKEN MIRAGE	14
LOSS OF VIRGINITY	24
SEXUAL IMMORALITY	32
SUICIDE AND DEPRESSION	42
ISOLATION	52
HOMOSEXUALITY	60
DELIVERANCE	70
CLOSING PRAYER	78
ROMANS ROAD	79
THE REASON I WRITE	80
"MY STORY BEGINS HERE..."	81
CONTACT THE AUTHOR	88

DIARY OF A HAITIAN CHURCH GIRL

MOLESTATION

"And the Lord, He is the One who goes before you. He will be with you; He will not leave you nor forsake you; do not fear nor be dismayed"

(Deuteronomy 31:8).

MOLESTATION

Growing up in church as a little girl, I always feared God. At the end of each day, I would go over in my mind how many wrongs *(sins)* I had done so I could make sure to ask God to forgive me. When I began experiencing the first darkness in my life, I began to ask, *"Where is my God? What did I do wrong?"* I **pleaded** to God to forgive me for whatever I had done to cause Him to let me go through the darkness.

I was like Jesus on the Cross on Calvary, asking, "Why have thou forsaken me?" (Matthew 27:46).

I was 11 years old. Around that time, there were many immigrants migrating to the United States - some for a better life; others simply wanted to touch the ground of U.S. soil.

MOLESTATION

*Our house was **always** full of people. We were living in a two-bed, two-bath complex. There were six people living with us, including people who were coming in and out for a place to sleep temporarily. A few were family members of my stepfather: his brothers, nephew, and so forth. I considered them my family since they were his.*

*I **never** considered any of them being the "creepy uncle", until being playful with one went too far.*

*I remember sitting in the living room watching television while some of the adults were outside or away from home. It was then that one man whom I considered my uncle touched me inappropriately. At the time, I didn't understand what he was doing, but I did know this: **It didn't feel right.***

DIARY OF A HAITIAN CHURCH GIRL

*I can clearly recall him making the **"Shh...Shh..."** sound, instructing me to be quiet. That first time was shocking, but when it happened several other times, **that** is when I knew it wasn't right at all.*

*Growing up in a 'Haitian' household, discipline was used as a scare tactic. Either your parents tried to scare you or beat you almost to death, all in an effort to make you who they wanted you to be or act the way they wanted you to act. "Telling" on an adult would be reason for disciplinary actions. They were the elders and could do "**no** wrong". Some would think, "At least she could tell her mom!" - and they would be **wrong**. Haitian parents made you afraid of them, and opening your mouth about something like molestation would bring complete chaos to the family...**or** you would be labeled a liar. So, I kept my mouth shut with my tears balled up inside, all the while asking, "Where is the God we sing and pray to daily?"*

MOLESTATION

Why would God allow me to go through that pain?

We can attack that subject a few ways:

1. The devil was at work; or
2. God allowed it to happen so that He could set me apart; or
3. There was a purpose to the pain experienced at an early age.

There is no doubt molestation is wrong. If it ever happens to you, **SPEAK UP!** What I don't want you to do is allow it to define who you are.

It is not uncommon for teenagers to not be able to see past the moment. I thought, *"Why would God cause someone to act like this towards a child?"*

We have this mindset that everyone is the same, when in fact there are different **spirits** residing in each person. Not everyone who attends church is attaching himself or herself to God. As children, we live by emotions and relationships. In my mind, that man was supposed to protect…not hurt. He was supposed to build up…not destroy. Be careful using your emotions because the enemy can cause you to perceive something or someone a certain way. You must look *beyond* that emotion and, instead, look underneath the surface.

When you feel the most 'alone' is when you feel God the most. He appears to let you know you are **not** alone. Because God is a Spirit, He can come in many different forms.

MOLESTATION

*One day, in my third-grade class, my teacher was teaching us about "good touch, bad touch" and what to do if bad touching happens. She told us if we **ever** experience anything bad, we can always come and tell her. She also said she will not let anyone know (or so I was led to believe). I decided to pull her aside one day after she assigned the class an activity to complete. I started to tell her **everything**: how it began, how it made me feel, who the person was, and where the person lived.*

In my mind, I thought it was over after I told her - but it was only the beginning.

I will never forget the day...

DIARY OF A HAITIAN CHURCH GIRL

*It was a Wednesday evening. I remember so well because it was the day the men of the church went to the field to practice playing soccer. I was sitting on the floor between my mother's legs as she combed my hair for school the next day. There was a knock at the door. It was already evening, and old-school Haitian parents did **not** tolerate guests after sunset.*

My mother got up and peered through the door viewer. I could see the fear in her eyes as she spoke out loud: "Sa polis sa yo ap fe devan pot kay mwen?" - *meaning* **"What are these police doing in front of my door?"**

MOLESTATION

She opened the door. The officers greeted her and asked to speak with me. They didn't come inside the house. Instead, they asked me to join them outside and had my mother close the door behind me. They explained that my teacher called and told them what was going on with me. They asked me if it was true, and I responded "yes". They asked me for the name of the person and if he was inside the house. I told them his name and explained he was out with the other men practicing soccer. When they were done speaking with me, they then spoke with my mother. She was not happy at all. Haitian mothers have a way of not saying a single word while cussing you out with their eyes and facial expressions.

*The police officers waited until the men arrived back at the house. As the men approached the door, each had to state his name. Once the "creepy uncle" stated his name, he was **immediately** handcuffed, read his rights, and told what he was being arrested for.*

DIARY OF A HAITIAN CHURCH GIRL

One would think I would have felt happy or relieved, but that was only the beginning of the isolation stage in my life.

My teacher was God's angel at that moment for me. I felt comfortable enough to open up to her after she taught us the "*good touch, bad touch*" lesson.

That is what the Word of God does for our soul as well. You hear it and it makes you feel **compelled** to move, confess, and release whatever is weighing you down.

What God **also** does after you hear the Word is place people in your path. They could be a pastor, prophet, neighbor…or even a stranger.

God uses His Holy Spirit to tell your business, but the people whom He tells it to are there to help you out of bondage. That is what my teacher did for me when she called the police.

MOLESTATION

One day, I asked her why she called the police after stating she would never tell anyone. She told me she **had** to because it would have continued if she didn't break the silence.

After the police left with him, everyone was in great shock. The one thing that hurt me the most was that no one - absolutely no one - was concerned about how I felt. No one asked me any questions about the situation. It was then I knew: **I was alone.** *As a child, it was the worst feeling ever to expect to be nurtured, but instead, those same people turned their backs on me when I needed them the most.*

As the days went by and the police were conducting their investigation, I was court-ordered to see a therapist. What the therapist didn't know was some of my family and church family were trying to persuade me to change my story. I was told to say I made up the story and that he never violated me.

No one *cared that my innocence was stolen; they only cared about that man's deportation. They decided to close their eyes and ears to a hurting child. Instead of thanking God that he would not be able to hurt other children, they decided to protect someone who brought harm instead of healing!*

Many people can relate to this *type* of experience in any type of relationship: familial, friendship, boyfriend/girlfriend, or church family. At times, you feel like you are part of a **family**, but when things go wrong or the darkness comes, there is **no one** there for you.

God has to place people in your life to change your environment, to help you pray, and to teach you how to do better. If not, you will remain stuck in the same mess.

"Train a child in the way he should go, and when he is old he will not depart from it"

(Proverbs 22:6).

BROKEN MIRAGE

Parents are who we form and build our morals and values from. Even the children who did not grow up with their parents have *at least* one person in their lives they look up to; a teacher, grandparent, another elder, neighbor, or an older sibling. We must be careful to not put them on an unreachable pedestal as if they could do 'no wrong'.

The fact remains: **We are all human.** The ultimate Father of all who can do **NO** wrong is our *Heavenly Father*. Growing up, we may not correlate God as being the Provider of all things. We typically rely on our parents or other guardians to receive emotional support. If not careful, they can *(at times)* **create** a void instead of filling one.

Generally speaking, there is a **serious** lack of affection in the Haitian household. To hear the words *'I love you'* or *'Good job'* is very rare. It makes children in the household look for affection and love in the wrong way and in wrong places.

What if I told you that all the love you are looking for can be found in God? He is the Father who will **never** forsake you. He will love you unconditionally with a love that overflows like a river.

I know, I know: Being human, you may need a hug from time to time. I believe God places people in your path - if even for a short time - and uses them to manifest Himself in order to get that physical hug you need or even some words of encouragement.

I wish I knew that growing up. I was not taught that in my "traditional church".

DIARY OF A HAITIAN CHURCH GIRL

*I found out my stepfather was not my **birth** father through pictures. I found a photo album my mother had hidden. On one of the pages, there was a picture of me as a baby being held by a man. It took a while before I could ask my mother about that picture, but eventually, I did. She explained to me that the man was my father. Her tone was uncaring and lacked concern for my feelings. I could tell she was **relieved** that she no longer had to keep that secret from me.*

*Mother described my father as someone who did not care for me. **All** respect was to be given to my stepfather because he was the one who was taking care of me - something I could partially agree with.*

BROKEN MIRAGE

Thoughts began racing through my mind about my birth father. Where was he? Why didn't he ever come to see me? Did he not love me? *My mother made me feel like he **never** wanted me just by the things she used to say, such as:*

*My father **never** took care of me as a baby.*

***She** was the one who struggled to take care of me.*

*My father **never** paid her child support.*

*The gut punch was when she said he **never** even asked to see me.*

Many Haitian parents fail to understand that as a child, their words impact and form the lives of the youths around them. Words can either build you up **or** break you down. The Word of God does the same. When God created Adam, He blessed him by using His *words*. God used *words* to speak life into Adam, instructing him to "*...be fruitful, multiply, replenish, and subdue on Earth*" (Genesis 1:28). God prepared Adam for the future.

The words that were said to me as a child about my father impacted the relationship between my father and I until this very day.

BROKEN MIRAGE

I will never forget the day I met my father for the first time. It was also the day I found out I had an older brother and a sister who was three months younger than me. I was 12 years old and preparing to go on a field trip with my school. I guess ever since the situation with the "creepy uncle", the money my stepfather gave my mother to take care of me started to decrease - although we were still living under the same roof. For that reason, my mother contacted my father to let him know I needed some items for the field trip.

*I remember being nervous, afraid, and excited all at the same time. I was about to meet the man I saw in those hidden photos - the man I used to hear **others** talk about.*

*He came to pick me up on a Saturday in his taxi. As I entered the car, he smiled. He didn't embrace me, but he **did** smile. He introduced me to my siblings and explained I was his second child but first girl. During the ride to Kmart (a quick 10-minute ride), I quickly got acquainted with my brother and sister. My brother was so cool and very down-to-earth. I felt so excited learning that I had an older sibling - one I could look up to. I remember thinking, "Now I have my family. I will no longer be alone and they would be there to defend me any time I was being mistreated".*

Reality quickly settled back in its place when I arrived back home and had to tell them 'good-bye'.

BROKEN MIRAGE

My brother and I stayed in contact for the rest of that school year and the Summer that followed. I remember us being on the phone with each other not saying a word while he would be playing video games with his friends. Just the fact that he was on the phone with me removed that feeling of constant loneliness that had found its place in my life.

At times, we need that **one** person who provides comfort simply by their presence - even if no words are spoken. Their presence makes us feel better and content. We must learn to be that person for another. That's what **God** wants us to do.

DIARY OF A HAITIAN CHURCH GIRL

When school started after Summer break, the phone calls with my brother soon became less and less. I began seeking attention elsewhere…and in the wrong way. I started to feel like the fairy tale character 'Cinderella' in our house. I was **always** washing, cleaning, lifting, and cooking *something*. Most would excuse it away as being the "Haitian culture" and that my mother was preparing me to become a woman, but what about that laundry list of *other* stuff that needed to be said and wasn't?

I am thankful for the teachings my mother provided on how to keep my home in order, but there were many more lessons that should have been taught. We need our parents to not be afraid of being more open with us. We need to hear and know they are human…just like us.

LOSS OF VIRGINITY

"Or do you not know that your body is the temple of the Holy Spirit who is in you, whom you have from God and you are not your own? For you were bought at a price; therefore, glorify God in your body and in your spirit, which are God's"
(1 Corinthians 6:19-20).

LOSS OF VIRGINITY

God states, "*The lack of knowledge causes His people to perish*" (Hosea 4:6).

I was perishing in front of people around me, but they could not help because they were not equipped to give me the knowledge they never had! *No one can feed you if they have no food for themselves.*

I was **never** taught about menstruation, sex, and other essential life topics. Because of the lack of information and teaching from home, I started reacting to the changes my body was going through. I lost my *innocence* at the age of 11 - but I lost my **virginity** at the age of 12. If I had the right teaching, then I would not have allowed those biological changes to have control over my *mind*. I would have understood that what I was feeling at the moment would pass.

LOSS OF VIRGINITY

When you spend time with God, you begin to realize that your body is a temple and you should not allow anyone to defile it. I believe your body is the most sacred part of you. You are supposed to give your body as a living sacrifice to **God**. We should not allow temporary enjoyment to take permanent place in our lives.

*I allowed a 16-year-old who lived across the street from me to enter in my holies of holies. He was the 'new kid on the block' and **all** the young girls liked him. I felt so special because he chose me.*

I will never forget the day I gave in to the changes that were happening inside of me....

DIARY OF A HAITIAN CHURCH GIRL

*My mother and stepfather owned a shoe store. Usually, I was sent to stay at the store on Saturdays. At the time, my mother was a cosmetologist. She would have to take care of her clients, and my stepfather had a full-time job. At times, he would have to work the weekend shift. Being the oldest child, I was sent to the store so that it would remain open and, of course, **to clean**. The 'new kid' would often come to the store and spend time with me.*

*He decided one day that "spending time" with me wasn't enough. He came in as usual one Saturday, walked behind the counter, and started kissing me. From kissing, he began to rub on my thighs. From there, whatever my flesh wanted, it received. I lost **all** control. All I remember was locking the front door of the store and entering the storage room in the back. He opened Pandora's Box - and once opened, it was **not** ready to close anytime soon.*

LOSS OF VIRGINITY

*After a few weeks of enjoying myself with the 'new kid', I found out I was not the **only** one he was enjoying. He broke my heart. All that I was able to do to comfort myself was listen to Toni Braxton's "Un-break My Heart"...repeatedly.*

The pain was **intense**. We - as children of God - must be equipped and prepared before making any decisions in our lives. We can end up derailing God's plans for us when we do not ask *Him* to guide us in our daily lives. When we do not adhere to God's guidance, the enemy has access to lead us in the wrong direction. Making wrong choices causes us to go through unnecessary suffering and brings **so** much brokenness. God is the **ONLY** one who can make us whole.

DIARY OF A HAITIAN CHURCH GIRL

I started looking for something or someone to take away the pain. I began dating a 19-year-old who *also* lived across the street from me. I opened myself up in that relationship and met with other people who were walking in darkness. I started to hang out with drug dealers and strippers. I was introduced to guns, crack, marijuana, and cocaine. I became part of a "trap house" *(a home used with the exclusive purpose of dealing drugs)* and did not even know it. I took so many chances with my life, but with the grace of God, I was never harmed nor arrested for **any** criminal activities.

You must be careful who you surround yourself with. Although I was never a stripper or sold drugs, people who did not *know* me looked at me in that light. I began to resemble those I was around. It is said, "*You are who you associate yourself with*".

LOSS OF VIRGINITY

The **BEST** person to associate yourself with is **GOD**. You can receive the blessings of Heaven and bear His fruits. You gain a Friend who *always* has your back - not one who will incriminate you just to save himself.

DIARY OF A HAITIAN CHURCH GIRL

SEXUAL IMMORALITY

"For this is the will of God, your sanctification: that you should abstain from sexual immorality; that each of you should know how to possess his own vessel in sanctification and honor"
(1 Thessalonians 4:3-4).

SEXUAL IMMORALITY

After getting used to a situation, you start looking for the next new and exciting thing. I started to think older men would treat me better. I started dating men who were a few years older than me. When those men were done using my body and then throwing me aside, I felt a part of me was left with them.

We are *spirits* that live inside a body. Each time we attach ourselves to or have sex with someone, we leave pieces of ourselves with that person. A person who has had many sexual partners becomes a lost spirit - one who does not know who he or she is nor where he or she is going. Each person who enters their lives becomes their identity. They begin to conform themselves to **that** person's lifestyle, personality, and demands. Not knowing who you are delays you in life.

SEXUAL IMMORALITY

God wants our spirits to be tied with Him and for us to find our identity in Him. **HE** created us to be a reflection of Him and to step into the purpose and destiny He has chosen for us. Because we fail to realize the value and importance of the breath of life He places inside of us (Genesis 2:7), we allow the wrong people to enter and change the image God has already placed on us.

It is common, but of course, some would be in denial in the Haitian community that teenage girls would be in a sexual relationship with older men. I am not saying it is right, but reality is this: *It happens.* Without God, we make naïve choices. I am guilty of doing just that.

DIARY OF A HAITIAN CHURCH GIRL

Teenagers who usually end up in situations like that are either looking for love they never had at home, someone to take care of them financially, or *(the most common reason)* because their father was not around. I had two or three of those reasons on lockdown!

I began dating men who were as old as my **parents**. There was something about dating those older men... They would look into my eyes as if to hypnotize me. At the time, I naively thought it was love, but it was really just lust. I did not have an understanding of the difference between love and lust. No one ever sat me down and talked to me about it. *How can we know if we are never taught?*

SEXUAL IMMORALITY

*I began a sexual relationship with a "community bus driver" and became very attached to him. I never had the habit of lying about my age, so he was **fully** aware I was only **15 years old** at the time. As crazy as it may sound, I thought I was going to spend a long time with that man. I actually dreamt of he and I raising a family. My mind was so far gone and my eyes were so blind, I could not see I was not ready to be someone's wife. I was too much of a child to take care of a grown man's needs. I couldn't see past the moment.*

DIARY OF A HAITIAN CHURCH GIRL

The enemy likes to dominate your mind and play games with it. God and the devil know the desires of everyone's heart. Satan uses them **against** you and manipulates it so that he can either kill you, destroy your future, or steal the destiny God has already spoken into your life (John 10:10). God looks at your desires and determines if they are good for you. If they **are** good for you, then He prepares you before giving them to you. You must *always* ask God for His wisdom to have a spirit of discernment so that when something or someone is presented to you, you are able to make the right decision.

Anyone who tries to persuade you pursues your mind first. They must first know what is in you. Once they know that, they cover up the seed they want to plant in your mind with something that is already in you. It may be something you like or a conviction you may have regarding a certain topic.

SEXUAL IMMORALITY

I started to spend a lot of time with the "community bus driver". I started sneaking out and sleeping away from home with him - sometimes **days** *at a time. Of course, my mother was outraged. At times, she would not be able to locate me and would call law enforcement to file a Missing Person's report. I wasn't concerned with how my mother was feeling. I became selfish, looking only for something that did not really exist in that man.*

One night, as I was sleeping at his house (after again giving my body to him), *there came a knock at the door. It was the middle of the night. We saw there were police cars just outside the window. We both began to panic. Many things raced through my mind:* How did my mother find me? How did she know who I was with? *I ran and hid in the bathroom as he went to answer the door.*

NOTE: If you are doing something and have to hide, then you should not be doing it.

When he answered the door, my mother, the police, **AND** *an ex-boyfriend of mine were there. It was then I knew who snitched on me. My ex heard in the streets who I was with and where the man lived. The police asked the man questions. Soon after, he invited them in to come and get me. They sent me home with my mother and arrested the man for statutory rape. Although my mother didn't want to press charges* (because she felt I was to blame and I likely enticed the man), *the state's attorney decided to continue with the charges due to the crime. He was obligated to pay restitution and is forever marked as a sex offender.*

Remember: The enemy comes to kill, steal, and destroy. If he cannot kill you, he will find a way to destroy your life (John 10:10).

SEXUAL IMMORALITY

Today, the enemy has left his mark on that man just because he was too blind to make the right decision and to know when danger appeared. God is the only one who can change the mark of the enemy in your life. Just by acknowledging him and confessing your sins, He is able to do the rest.

You must ask God for the spirit of discernment. Don't **rush** to agree with something that someone asks you to do. Don't **rush** to act on an emotion or behavior of someone else. Doing so can very well be a trap the enemy prepared for you to fall into...

You will then become the "blind leading the blind" or the "pot calling the kettle black". We must ask **God** to lead us by *His Spirit* and understanding - not our own. When you allow that to happen, the enemy has no chance of marking **YOU** as his territory.

DIARY OF A HAITIAN CHURCH GIRL

SUICIDE AND DEPRESSION

"For you are my lamp, O Lord; the Lord shall enlighten my darkness"
(2 Samuel 22:29).

SUICIDE AND DEPRESSION

What is 'depression'? Clinicians would say it is caused by chemical changes in the brain. I say depression is darkness - a darkness the **devil** created just for you to stop you from seeing the sunshine behind the clouds. The enemy blurs your vision so that you remain stuck looking at the dark clouds for so long, you forget the sunshine is coming.

I want to make it clear: Depression is not **FROM** God nor **OF** God. *What type of God would He be if He wanted you to be sad all the time?* One of the spiritual fruits of God is **"JOY"** (Galatians 5:22-23). Nowhere in the scriptures is *sadness* included as a fruit of the Spirit.

SUICIDE AND DEPRESSION

It is okay to feel sad about a situation, but it is how long you allow the situation to affect you that makes the difference. You must look at every situation for the moment and ask God what He wants you to learn from it. *What is causing you to feel the way you feel?*

*I suffered from depression for many years, to the point I attempted suicide…**twice**. The first time I actually recognized depression had control of my life was when I was 17 years old. I didn't want to get out of bed and I cried uncontrollably without cause. At times, I didn't even want to shower or speak to anyone. It became so severe, I disconnected from my family. I stopped attending family events because I did not want to be around people.*

Depression took a hold of my life again in my 20s. I began seeing a therapist and psychiatrist. I was diagnosed with chronic depression and began taking antidepressants to try to maintain my sanity.

Imagine living life without any emotions. Imagine living life not enjoying and appreciating the colorful moments in life. That is how my life was while taking the medication. My life lacked color because I was not **'LIVING'**!

If you are dealing with the negative effects of depression on *any* level, I want you to ask yourself this question: *Is that truly the way God wants you to live?* **Of course not!** So, why would you **choose** to live that way?

Any time I stopped taking the antidepressant, I was left with an overwhelming sadness. The medication became bondage while I was in the prison of depression - being bound and unable to move past the prison wall.

SUICIDE AND DEPRESSION

*My first attempt at suicide was when I was 16 years old. There were no specific reasons that caused me to do it on **THAT** particular day. It was just a "build up" of days of being depressed. I was hearing voices and having thoughts that were telling me there was no reason for me to be alive...no one loved me. I kept hearing,* **"You don't have value. You are not pretty enough. There's no place in this world for you."**

Those are tricks of the devil! The enemy plays with your mind just like that. He takes the Word of God and flips it to have you do what *he* wants you to do. While you are in his prison, he feeds you whatever he wants you to have. He continues to feed you things you don't like about yourself in order to remove the hope and peace within.

I will prove it to you.

DIARY OF A HAITIAN CHURCH GIRL

Satan says: "*There is no place in this world for you.*"

GOD says: **"*For I know the thoughts that I think toward you, says the LORD; thoughts of peace and not of evil, to give you a future and a hope*"** (Jeremiah 29:11).

Satan says: "*You are not pretty enough.*"

GOD says: **"*I will praise you for I am fearfully and wonderfully made; marvelous are your works and that my soul knows very well*"** (Psalms 139:14).

Satan says: "*There is no reason for you to be alive.*"

GOD says: **"*And he has made from one blood every nation of men to dwell on all the face of the Earth, and has determined their preappointed times and the boundaries of their dwellings*"** (Acts 17:26).

SUICIDE AND DEPRESSION

Satan says: "*No one loves you.*"

GOD says: *"For God so loved the world, that He gave His only begotten Son, that whoever believes in Him should not perish but have everlasting life"* (John 3:16).

You see, the enemy knows the Word of God very well. He knows it **so** well, he twists it to his own benefit. **You** must *know* the Word of God as well in order to give a rebuttal when the enemy says something untrue about you.

Depression is a spirit from the devil and must be fought with the Word of God. Grab your sword and cut the devil where it hurts the most!

When all those thoughts came over me, I was at my stepfather's home. As I took the bottle of pills, tears were streaming down my face. All I wanted to do was die peacefully. My stepfather came looking for me. When he found me, I was laid out on the bed with an empty pill bottle nearby and speaking with slurred speech. He **immediately** recognized what was going on. He sat me up and created a home-remedy that caused me to vomit what was inside of me. He stayed awake and kept watch over me all throughout the night to be sure all was well with me.

My second suicide attempt was when I was 18 years old. My husband at the time was **very** aware of my depressed state of mind. He called it "acting crazy" because he could not understand my 'why' and reason for depression. I had no obvious reason to have that mindset, so to him, it made no sense.

SUICIDE AND DEPRESSION

No one can understand the way you feel - except you and God. It doesn't make sense to others…and it pains those who love you. Someone outside looking in does not understand the tight grip the enemy has on you.

I locked myself in the bathroom, sat in a tub full of water, and swallowed not one, but **TWO** *full bottles of pills. 'Til this day, I* **still** *do not know how my husband knew something was wrong. He banged on the door. When I did not answer, he knocked the door down, removed me from the tub, and placed me on the floor.*

All I can remember is him yelling at me asking me what I was doing and thinking. All glory be to **GOD***: I didn't have to go to the hospital. All glory be to* **GOD***: I lacked nothing after the attempt. Depression had taken over my life, and no one who was around me knew how to deal with it nor how to help me get rid of it.*

You must surround yourself with people who have a light shining from within. They can hold their "flashlight" when the battery in yours dies while walking through the darkness. Don't accept stubbing your toes on the leg of the bedpost, **especially** if you have someone there who is willing to hold the light for you as you walk.

ISOLATION

"But you are a chosen generation, a royal priesthood, a holy nation, His own special people, that you may proclaim that praises of Him who called you out of darkness into His marvelous light"

(1 Peter 2:9).

ISOLATION

At one point or another in our lives, we have **all** felt as if we did not 'fit in' - even as adults. *What if I told you* **GOD** *created you just the way you are?*

I will admit: I was the chubby, Haitian nerd with a book in my hand...*always*. Even though I knew most of the popular kids in school *(because they lived in my neighborhood)*, I was never part of "the in-crowd". I grew up being apart from others. No one took a chance to get to know me to try to relate to me.

"Then God said, "Let us make man in Our image, according to Our likeness..." (Genesis 1:26).

The question to ask yourself is this: *What is God's image?* The answer is this: God's image is in **EVERYONE'S** image!

I'll just let that marinate in your spirit for a minute...

ISOLATION

Every single person has a part of God in them. He is **SO** big, our minds do not have the capacity to even *BEGIN* to imagine all that God is capable of. Each of us possesses a different creative gift; either doing hair, nail graphics, playing music, singing, writing, sewing or even being able to use words in an articulate way. **ALL** of those things and more are inside of God! He contains *everything* inside of Him and gives each of us a piece.

I did not know that growing up, so I wanted to share that with **you** *now*. Don't try to fit into a **manmade** box or group of people to feel like you 'belong'.

DIARY OF A HAITIAN CHURCH GIRL

I **loved** school. In middle school, I was enrolled in honor classes. I enjoyed learning new things and using my mind to excel. I was not perfect in school, though. Everyone has a weakness - and mine was math. Because I felt out of place amongst my own schoolmates, I would often skip classes. I thought high school would have gotten better. No. It was **worse**! I gained weight the Summer before starting my 9th-grade year. I was not able to fit into the nice, cute outfits all the girls were going to wear. I was excited when I was accepted at a magnet school because I thought I would have been around people who were 'like me'.

I started school with excitement, but that joy quickly died when I realized I knew **no one** there and was not able to make friends. Eating lunch alone can be a very lonely experience, especially without someone even **pretending** to be your friend. Well, in response to the lack of attention, I started skipping classes there - and eventually got kicked out of that school.

ISOLATION

*My mother decided to register me in the neighborhood public high school. A majority of the people from middle school attended that school. I thought for **sure** I was going to have a social life because people would know me. After all, we were mature high-schoolers (at least in our own minds). I really tried my best to fit in. I tried making myself more approachable. Then, I started noticing some people would speak to me **IN** class but not **OUTSIDE** of class. It started to affect me so bad on the inside, I came to believe that no one in the **WORLD** liked me. The rush of pain that started when I was 11 years old took over my life and led me on a path of destruction.*

DIARY OF A HAITIAN CHURCH GIRL

Far too many Haitian parents do not understand *(or they simply don't try to understand)* the pains their children endure - not only in school, but in this world. The adults make a decision to dismiss their children's cries for help. They believe only disciplinary actions will 'fix it', but they rarely take the time to talk about or ask, *"What's the problem?"*

I was **crying** for help - not with my words, but with my actions.

I couldn't take it anymore. I didn't fit in at home. I didn't fit in at school. I started to think, "What is the point of living? What was my purpose of being here?" When it becomes too painful living on Earth, you find yourself asking God, **"Why would you create a place like this?"**

ISOLATION

*I was hurting...immensely. I cried **every** night, wishing the day was night - and when night came, I was wishing it was day. I decided to drop out of high school in the 9th grade and started roaming the streets. I stopped reading. I stopped writing. I was barely eating and started smoking marijuana. I gave up on life and decided I was going to live from house to house...with men. It is **ONLY** by the grace of God that I am able to stand and say I beat the statistics. I didn't become a homeless, uneducated female with some incurable disease.*

As individuals, we each have a responsibility to assure one another that we are loved - despite our differences. We are **ALL** God's creation. He wants us to love one another **MORE** than we love ourselves (Mark 12:31). *Can you imagine if we all abided by that Word?* No one would feel out of place. Like a potter with his clay, God uniquely designed each of us. *What right do we have to say to someone they are not good enough?* All clays are formed with a purpose in mind: for someone to eat on, drink from…or to plant in. Think about it.

Once you find yourself in God's presence and stronghold, all of what others say does not matter because you have found your identity in Him. You are who **GOD** says you are. The only way to find out who He says you are is by reading His book - the Holy Bible - and having a one-on-one relationship with Him.

HOMOSEXUALITY

> *"And even as they did not like to retain God in their knowledge, God gave them over to a debased mind, to do those things which are not fitting"*
> (Romans 1:28).

HOMOSEXUALITY

The Holy Bible is a manual written by man - but *inspired* by God. Meditate on His Word and see what comes to mind. Whatever you are inspired by is what leads you.

God does **NOT** inspire homosexuality. That is not who or what He created you to be. I know this may be a sensitive topic, but the truth needs to be told. I have said it before and will say it again: Your true self is the spirit *within* - not the flesh. If each of us are spirits, then that means there are different types **AND** multiple spirits all around that are looking for a vessel to enter.

The purpose of this chapter is to expose the enemy's lies and deceits. This is not intended to judge or isolate **anyone**; rather it is to help you understand why God formed you and what needs to be changed in your life.

HOMOSEXUALITY

God's love is unconditional and meant for everyone. That is why He says He came to bring **LIFE** to all who believe in Him (John 10:10). *How can He not love us?* **He was the One who created us!**

I want to give you something - a nugget - to help you find your true identity in God...not what the *enemy* would have you believe. Although you may feel comfortable in your situation, it does not mean that is where you are **supposed** to be nor who you really are.

COMFORT IS CONFORMITY.

Being worried about what is around you and what people think about you makes you adjust yourself to not be different...to not stand out in the 'crowd'.

DIARY OF A HAITIAN CHURCH GIRL

The first time I realized I was attracted to the same sex was when I was 16 years old - which means *(simply put)*: **I was NOT born that way.** At the time, I didn't know where the attraction came from, but as I started to become one with God, He began revealing things to me. It's amazing what God will show you in order to make you stronger or for you to learn from your mistakes.

*My mother sent me to Job Corps in order to get me away from my toxic environment **and** so that I could get a high school diploma (since I decided to drop out of high school). I lived in an all-girl dorm that had four hallways. Each hallway had four to five rooms, and each room housed at least five people. The dorm I was in was known as the "lesbian and promiscuous dorm". I was surrounded by a diverse group of females with different backgrounds coming from different environments.*

HOMOSEXUALITY

The girls in the dorm started sleeping with each other. Those who were already used to sleeping with women were introducing that lifestyle to others. Although I was not involved with any of the girls in the dorm, I was in their environment and was **witness** *to their activities. I started to subdue to the attraction of women.*

Even if something may appear to be the norm to those around you, you must **not** conform to it. God created you to be set apart so that *He* is able to nurture you (Romans 12:2).

If you are in a room with loud noises and music blaring, how can you hear from someone seated right next to you? If you are conforming to things around you, that means you are not able to hear from God. You can only hear those around you!

The question you should ask yourself is this: *Why and how did those feelings come over me if I never had them before?* The answer is this: People who had those spirits in them became part of your environment - and mine. Trust me when I say: **I had front row seats to see all that was going on around me.**

The eyes are windows to the soul. What we see creates an image in our mind. It is a lot like watching a movie. When you fall asleep, the movie is replayed in your mind while you slumber. Whatever images are in your mind stick to you. Those images will, in turn, begin to manifest on the outside. Your thoughts become your emotions. Your emotions become your actions. You must protect yourself from what you see and the environment you are exposed to.

HOMOSEXUALITY

*As years went by, my attraction for women increased. I was 19 years old when I had my **first** sexual encounter with a woman. It was a coworker. She made it clear she was openly gay, but I befriended her anyway. We became close friends. I began spending time at her home. Her environment became my environment. I slept over her house while her mom was out of state. As we laid next to each other one night, something came over me. My mind and the attraction for a woman's body started to take over. I started to envision how it would feel to have my body up against hers.*

DIARY OF A HAITIAN CHURCH GIRL

While she was sleeping, I kissed her. I had never kissed a woman before, but my flesh enjoyed it. She didn't respond at first. I could've - I probably should've - stopped there, but I didn't. I kissed her again and she woke up. She awakened as if she was expecting it...expecting me. Kissing led to me opening my whole self to her. That began our year-long relationship. It was not a blissful year for me. The relationship brought a lot of pain, shame, and embarrassment. As well, because of the relationship, I lost my job.

HOMOSEXUALITY

The people we keep company with says a lot about who we **truly** are. We hang around people who are like us or who we aspire to become. As I reflect back on that relationship, I realized I subconsciously befriended that person based on what I wanted and what was in her. That means the *spirit* within me was already low-key and decided to manifest itself by becoming attracted to the spirit of homosexuality that was within her. I hid that relationship from a lot of people who knew me from before because I was ashamed.

MESSAGE
WHATEVER GOD HAS FOR YOU, YOU WILL *NEVER* BE ASHAMED OF IT!

That was my first and last relationship with a woman; however, my attraction for them continued. I started noticing everything in my surroundings was based on that lifestyle. My friends and travels in that 'circle' continued after the relationship itself was over. Only when I gave my life over to God and asked Him to cleanse me from my past sins was I able to stop having sexual desires for women.

Perhaps your story is different from mine. Maybe you have found yourself in a similar situation. I want you to **really** analyze the who, what, when, where, and why of that lifestyle. If you are ready for God to deliver you *(and I pray you are)*, He will do so - if you are a **willing** vessel. It may take some time, but don't stop seeking God's guidance, face, and forgiveness.

All things are possible with God (Matthew 19:26).

DELIVERANCE

"If we confess our sins, He is faithful and just to forgive us our sins and to cleanse us from all unrighteousness"
(1 John 1:9).

DELIVERANCE

As long as we are obedient and willing, God can do *marvelous* things in us in spite of our past. You may be able to relate to one or more of my tribulations discussed in this book, but rest assured: **God can change it to work best in your *favor*!**

Satan is here to rob you of the garment God has already placed on you. With each dimension of your life, God is able to give you a new and brighter garment each time. I am able to stand and say that I am **DELIVERED** and **FREED** from my past. My past no longer has a hold on my future!

DELIVERANCE

Life is a journey. It took some time for me to get to this point - and I have yet to reach the 'Finish' line. The enemy always tries to hold your past against you to make you feel as if God can **never** use you for His kingdom, but there are many people in the Bible with a **HORRIBLE** past who God used to glorify *His* name.

Moses was a murderer. **God** used him to lead the people of Israel out of Egypt.

Jacob was a trickster and a scammer. **God** used him to father a nation.

Paul was a killer of Christians. **God** used him greatly to spread the gospel and inspired him to write several books in the Bible.

We are ALL reusable by God.

DIARY OF A HAITIAN CHURCH GIRL

I am not going to try and fool you: The walk with God is not an *easy* one. It is hard and, at times, painful - but if you persevere and endure, He will make sure you lack **nothing** (James 1:4). God has placed power in your hands to overcome the enemy's temptations, attacks, and ill-devised strategies against you. God has given us our rights and dominion to trample on the enemy's head and to arrest the enemy for the crimes he has committed toward us. The more time you spend reading God's Word, the more He will enlighten your mind to know how to stop the enemy dead in his tracks.

You may have feelings of not wanting to live in this world any longer, but trust and believe this: *God created you for a purpose. You are a part of His plan!* We are **all** pieces of His puzzle and, at the end, you will be able to see the picture in its entirety and see how you were the **perfect** fit.

DELIVERANCE

I remember sitting and thinking: *There has to be **something** more than me just living day to day.* God has since shown me He did not create me just to walk on His Earth; He created me with a purpose to do His will - not my own. He created me to be a reflection of His love, His work, and **HIM**!

God knows **ALL**! Whenever we fall, He already knew we were going to. Whatever we are going through, He already knows about it. Temptations may come, but God has already created a gateway to escape. That gateway is found through *prayer*. Ask Him for strength to hold on to Him as He is holding on to you.

Remember this: *Whatever God allows, He has a plan - even if we cannot see it in the moment.*

I come not to judge. I am here to help guide the lost people of God and bring them back home to the sheepfold…to **HIM**. We are all His people, regardless of what we have done or said. Your environment may make you *FEEL* as if there is **NO WAY** God will forgive you, but He is a forgiving God! Trust me: There is much more to me than what is penned on the pages of this book, yet God decided to use me to bring forth a message on each of the aforementioned topics *specifically*. I encourage you to open up and let Him have access to your mind and body - His temple - so that He can do His mighty work in you.

DELIVERANCE

I want you to take some time and meditate on your current lifestyle. Be honest with yourself. Ask the hard questions:

Am I really where God wants me to be?

Am I really pleasing God?

Who is inspiring my thoughts, actions, and words?

Who has control over my future?

I want to encourage and bring light to you. Let's both walk out of the darkness…together.

This book is for those who feel like they are misunderstood. This book is for those who are suffering in silence. This book is for those who may feel that no one knows their pain.

God wants me to tell you He understands and feels your pain.

DIARY OF A HAITIAN CHURCH GIRL

CLOSING PRAYER

CLOSING PRAYER

Father,

Set your people free from the prison of the enemy. Show them the **GREATNESS** of you. Teach them not to lean on their own understanding, but to seek you daily. Help them recognize you sent your Son to purchase them at a price - and they owe the devil *nothing*. Build them up and use them to build up others. Show them your unconditional love and make them feel your presence. Place on them the white robe to remind them that the past is gone and that their sins have been forgiven.

This is a request sent to you from their Sister-in-Christ.

In Jesus' name, I pray.

Amen.

ROMANS ROAD

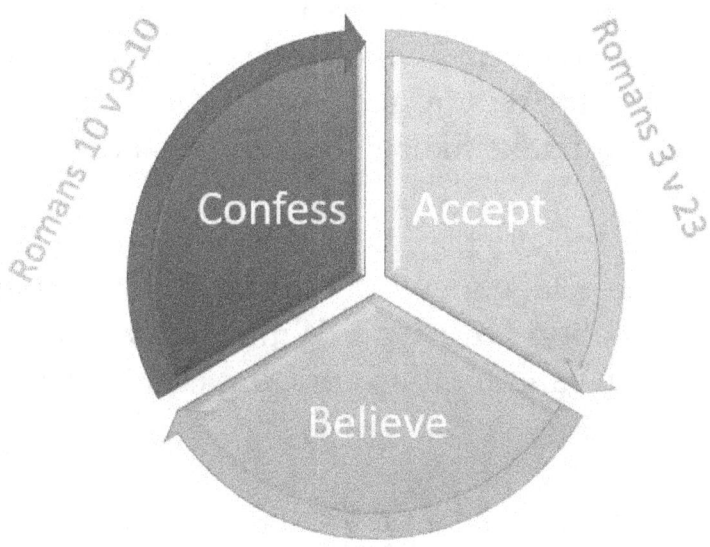

THE REASON I WRITE

I write because God speaks to me through writing. I write because I can make sense of the people and situations around me. Others may attempt to silence my voice to try to stop me from speaking my truth, but no one can take the pen out of my hand!

In a world full of chaos and noise, it can be hard at times to hear God's voice. Writing can be a part of your meditation with God. With each stroke of the pen in your hand, you are moving closer and closer to God.

All things are not meant to be shared with the public. Some things are only between you and the Creator. Take the time to write whatever you feel or may be going through. Write about your fears, joys, worries, questions, revelations, and your hopes for the future.

Writing is your voice! USE IT!

MY STORY BEGINS HERE

"My Story Begins Here..."

MY STORY BEGINS HERE

MY STORY BEGINS HERE

MY STORY BEGINS HERE

MY STORY BEGINS HERE

MY STORY BEGINS HERE

MY STORY BEGINS HERE

CONTACT THE AUTHOR

www.facebook.com/DiaryofAHaitianChurchGirl

Alexandra.Esperance@yahoo.com

www.ingramcontent.com/pod-product-compliance
Lightning Source LLC
Chambersburg PA
CBHW071531080526
44588CB00011B/1641